AUSTRALIA

reef, rainforest, red heart

AUSTRALIA

reef, rainforest, red heart

DARREN JEW

NEW HOLLAND

INTRODUCTION

Some places attract adventurous spirits. They are usually worlds defined by geography rather than arbitrary boundaries, regions into which we retreat to experience a landscape. These are the places that offer to quench our desire to explore and satisfy our yearning for space. They beckon the traveller and welcome the inquiring mind. With its life and landscape the product of ancient isolation, Australia is such a place.

For those who venture here, the experience begins long before their first footprint marks outback soil. Magazines, documentaries, the cinema play a part in moulding a collective impression of a mysterious continent rich in ecological diversity. While images of azure seas, lofty forests and sculpted deserts don't encompass the gamut of Australian nature, the reef, rainforest, red heart adventure is deeply rooted in many minds as the quintessential Australian experience.

On the outer Barrier Reef you could be the first to dive in an unexplored canyon. In the forests of the east coast ranges you may find plants and animals that scientists are yet to describe. You might travel for days across the arid outback without disturbing another soul. Everyone has their own motivation compelling them to explore the reefs, forests and interior of Australia. Some search for refuge from familiar surrounds, places of solitude and reflection, while others find that the passage itself is satisfaction enough. For everyone the journey leads to discovery and the fulfilment of long-held desires to be part of the place.

Faced with a flurry of new encounters, travellers may find their perceptions of a place are only superficial. The qualities that nourish a deeper response are found in more intimate experiences: textures of parched earth crackling under foot; pungent odours rising in the wake of a summer storm; the soft touch of wind disturbing a silent plain at dusk. Such moments nurture a sense of belonging, and lead us to find our place within a landscape. Without soaking up these subtle experiences, one really only visits.

My career has led me to some of Australia's remarkable places. I've learned about Australia from working closely with biologists on the reef, alongside park rangers in the mountains, and from myself as I've wandered alone in the desert. Experiencing this continent as traveller and photographer has left lasting impressions of complex landscapes and their myriad inhabitants, and has sparked a desire to share some of my images of this land.

With this book, I'd like to take you on a visual journey through three of this continent's most varied and remarkable ecosystems. We'll travel from the east coast, across the Great Dividing Range and westward toward the arid interior — and along the way we'll uncover some of the more subtle facets shaping the Australian experience.

reef

Our journey starts just off the north-east coast of Australia, in the warm and shallow waters of the continental shelf. It's here where, over the past 18 million years, reef-building corals have been laying down the largest coral reef complex on earth. Encompassing an area of 350 000 square kilometres, the Great Barrier Reef stretches from its northern extent near Papua New Guinea (about 10°S), over 2000 kilometres south to Lady Elliot Island (at 24°30'S). It is a labyrinth of individual reefs, islands and channels easily seen from space. A place still evolving as new corals thrive and the elements shape debris into sandbanks and, over time, into self-sufficient islands.

As the name suggests, the reefs form a barrier between the Coral Sea and the coast of north-eastern Australia. The coral structures lying close to the coast in the northern parts of the reef are the oldest, while toward the southern end, where the continental shelf is wider, reefs range from 50 to 300 kilometres offshore and are thought to be no more than two million years old.

The Great Barrier Reef is a relatively young Australian feature when compared with the tropical rainforests of the north of the continent and the ancient ranges and rivers of the interior. Yet in a relatively brief period it has become by far the most biologically diverse ecosystem on our planet, with its marine environment home to over 500 species of coral, 1500 species of fish, countless invertebrates, as well as sea turtles patrolling the lagoons and migrating whales over-wintering in warm reef waters. Above the surface, 19 of the 29 species of seabird found in the region descend on the reef's coral islands for the breeding season — creating a summertime flurry of millions of birds.

While the Great Barrier Reef is an impressive place, no statistics can convey the feeling of being there. More than in other places, a profound sense of escape is ever present on the reef. Maybe the expanse of sea between reef and mainland severs you physically and emotionally from places more familiar. Here you can walk on beaches of pure white coral sand under warm tropical sun and listen to the tinkle of coral rubble washed by clear, gentle shore breaks. This is a place where you can wonder at the precise manoeuvring of tail feathers and wingtips as squadrons of seabirds vie for position on unseen air currents; a place where the donning of mask and snorkel will suddenly replace terrestrial sounds and avian clamour with an inky silence and the wonder of all things new and marine.

rainforest

In an era of tropical rainforest domination around 120 million years ago, the southern hemisphere's supercontinent of Gondwana began to break up. Over the next 70 million years, the landmasses of Africa, India, South America, Antarctica and Australia separated and drifted toward their present positions, taking with them relics of these vast forests. Our planet has dried and cooled in the subsequent period and those rainforests have evolved into the various forms now found in scattered patches on each continent.

Today in warm, often wet, north Queensland, you can walk through tropical rainforest that has remained essentially unchanged throughout 50 million years of changing climate. These rainforests cling to the coast and ranges from Townsville to Cooktown, covering an area of just 7500 square kilometres, where soils, temperature and adequate rainfall support a unique rainforest time-capsule. The species diversity they hold in their flora and fauna is unmatched by any younger forest.

Patterns change as you move south into cooler regions, and subtropical rainforest begins to dominate the ranges where rainfall and soils are suitable. While not as diverse as their tropical cousins, these forests still hold a wealth of plant and animal life, including some Gondwanan relics and many species that have evolved in isolation. In common with their northern counterparts, the range of these forests is very limited — around 6000 square kilometres — or less than 0.1 per cent of the continent. While much of this area is now protected as permanent park, it is estimated that in the 200 years since European settlement, two-thirds of Australia's rainforests have been cleared for agriculture, logging and other development.

On an overcast day, without the confusion of dappled sunlight and deep shadows, you can see far into the forest. Silent vantages yield curious forest creatures. Beneath the leaf litter, an army of tiny life is intent on reducing plant material to soil. Rustling leaves and branches far above pre-empt the passage of the wind. Rain falls for minutes before reaching the forest floor, layers of foliage slowing each drop's progress. In this place you can listen to the land.

red heart

Travelling west from the coastal ranges, dramatic changes in landscape and vegetation become immediately apparent. Moist onshore air has dumped its load on the coastal plains, foothills and mountains. Clouds have all but dried up by the time they reach the western slopes. To travel further west is to begin to experience the fabled Australian bush — first the ubiquitous eucalypt forests, then through broad tracts of acacia woodland and across the arid plains of the interior.

Fossil and geological records show that prior to the start of northward continental drift about 50 million years ago, the centre of Australia was at times covered by a vast inland sea. During the same period that remnant rainforests were being isolated along the east coast, the central heart of Australia began drying out. While a few plant species that are relics of wetter times remain hidden in isolated pockets, essentially the interior of Australia is now a region containing a wealth of unique fauna and flora that has evolved to be perfectly adapted to life in harsh environs. Today Australia is over two-thirds arid land, and with much of it receiving less than 250 millimetres of rain each year, it is the driest habitable continent on earth.

The red centre provides the most obvious measures of the ancient nature of the continent. Here you can explore 1800 million years of geological history exposed in ancient riverbeds. It's a place where over the last 400 million years, ranges the size of the Canadian Rockies have been weathered down to mere folds on the plains.

When asked to visualise Australia, an alluring image of the outback is often the immediate response. We picture mobs of kangaroos bounding through grassy woodlands and weathered red rock sculptures rising from spinifex plains; a timeless land of big skies and unending horizons; a place where you can retreat to the summit of a rocky escarpment, gaze across a trackless landscape and surround yourself in uncompromising silence.

From above, the Great Barrier Reef reveals itself
as a splendid palette of texture...

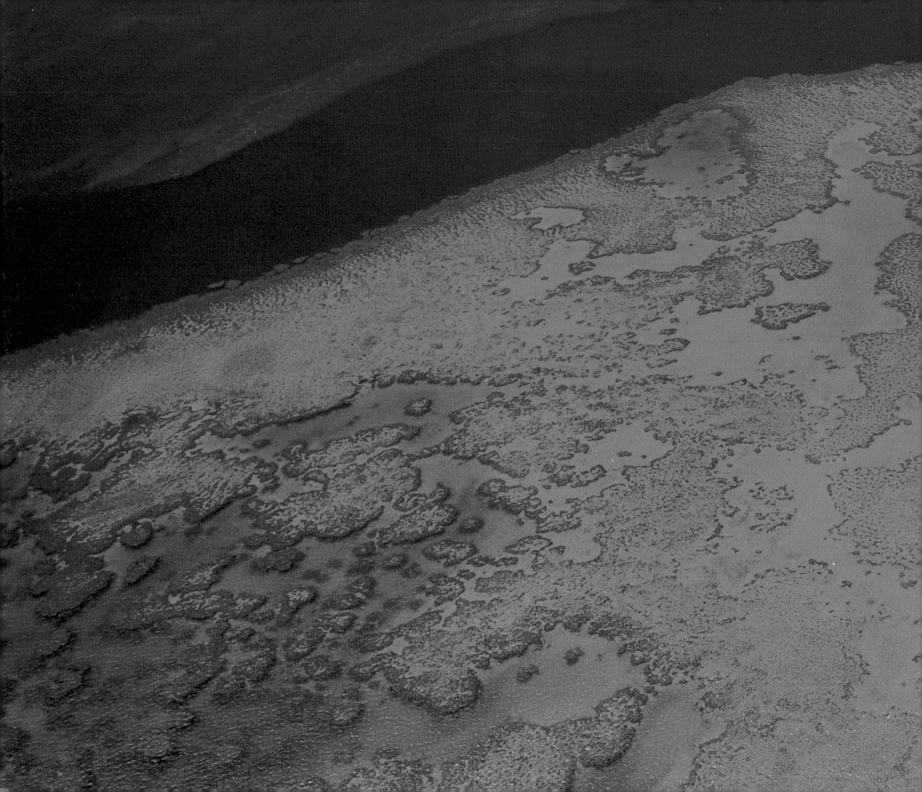

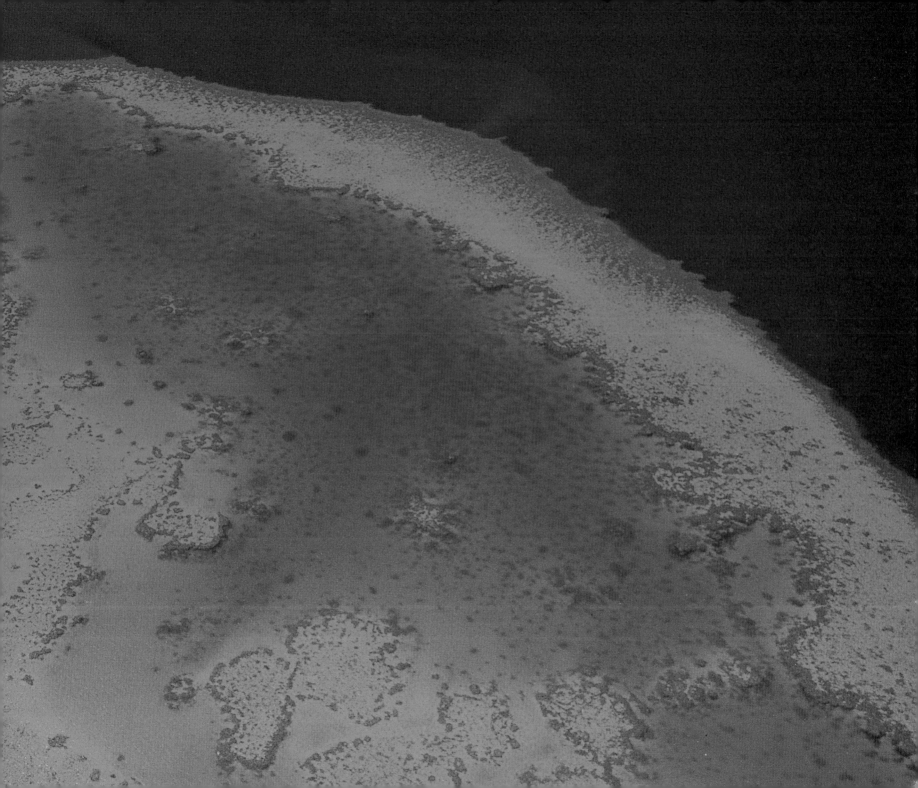

Rather than being a single reef, it is in fact a complex of countless smaller reefs, some of which support coral islands or cays. The silver-eye is a terrestrial bird sustained by the forests of developed cays.

The summer breeding season brings an influx of seabird life to the cays. While white-capped noddies nest in trees, crested terns gather in large breeding colonies on patches of open ground.

Beneath the surface, artificial light reveals colours otherwise subdued by the light-filtering
properties of seawater. In the shallows near the reef edge, corals
grow low and strong.

Reefs grow when calcium excretions from coral polyps produce a limestone skeleton.
In deep water, away from harsh wave action, delicate gorgonian fan corals spread out across
the current to filter nutrients from the sea.

The constant battering of wave action attests to the strength of reef building corals.
During the day, nocturnal species such as the sweetlip shelter in caves and under ledges of
limestone encrusted with new life.

Fish species have adapted different methods to deal with their predators. Batfish 'school' to confuse their predators, while anemone fish shelter amongst the poisonous tentacles of their host. The channels of open water between individual reefs are the realm of many schooling species, such as the trevally…

A school of baitfish moves as one through the sea. Barracuda cruise the channels in search of prey.

Above the waters of the reef life is also abundant. Crested terns court on the shore and predatory birds like the reef heron scour the reef flat for morsels.

Young frigatebirds mature into opportunists, stealing prey from other seabirds
rather than catching their own. Wind is the friend of most seabirds, so on
still days some species rest on the calm seas.

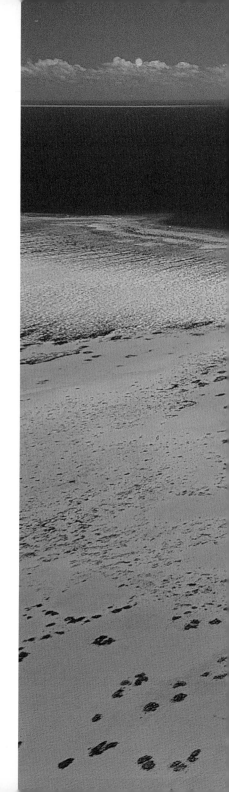

With a wingspan of over 1.5 metres, the brown booby soars easily over the reef life below. As a reef develops, wind and water erode coral rubble into sand and a cay begins to develop.

Tidal movements and storms gather the sand into sandbanks, providing a new habitat for reef life. Over time, nesting birds deposit nutrients and seeds, and the sandbank develops into a forested cay.

As the tide ebbs, the reef flat is exposed to reveal shallows teaming with intertidal life, which includes corals, algae, sea cucumbers and brilliant starfish.

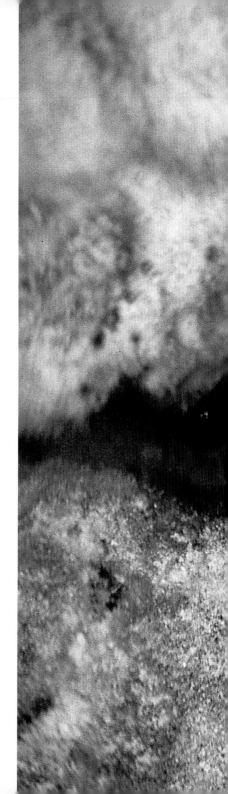

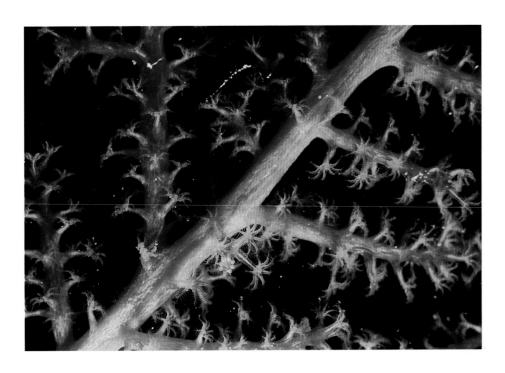

As night approaches light levels fall on the reef. Inactive by day, flowery polyps emerge from limestone branches and begin feeding.

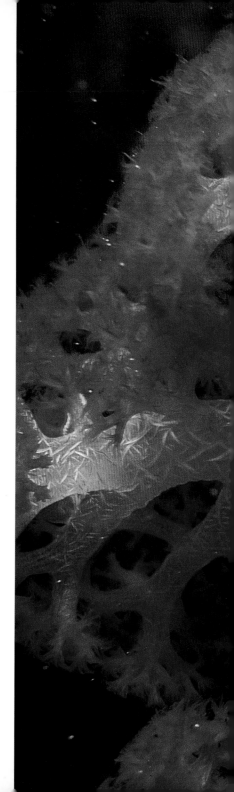

Thousands of tiny polyps create both hard and soft coral structures. Soft corals are colourful species that don't manufacture the characteristic reef-building skeleton of hard corals.

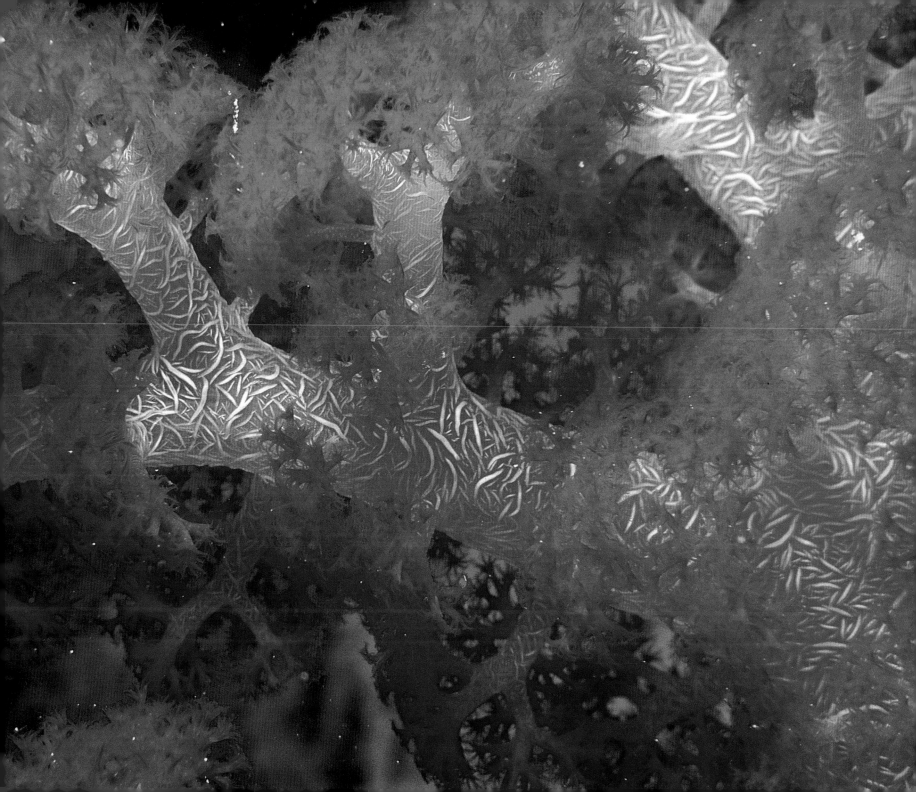

A female turtle returns to the sea after a night spent digging her nest and laying around 100 eggs. Cooling sands will trigger the emergence of tiny hatchlings about eight weeks after having been laid. Research shows that only one per cent of hatchlings survive to maturity.

Tracks are the only evidence of a female turtle's night of labour. It is understood that turtles return to lay their eggs at the beach of their birth. Rays patrol the shallows as day begins.

Following the line of the continental shelf, thousands of reefs and islands form an offshore barrier between the coast of north-east Australia and the Coral Sea.

Humpback whales can measure up to 15 metres in length and weigh over 40 tonnes. In winter they migrate to the warm waters inside the reef, their journey bringing them 6000 kilometres north from their Antarctic feeding grounds.

Humpbacks use the warm, shallow waters of the continental shelf to rest, mate and rear their young before following the coastline south again in the spring.

Continental islands are those that were formed when rising sea levels flooded coastal ranges.
The present-day shoreline is thought to be around 6000 years old.

Rocky headlands are the cornerstones of a coastline's stability. Here, permanent rock pools house their own mini ecosystems.

Away from the protection of barrier islands and reefs, the coast is punished by ocean swells.
Sandy coasts are at the mercy of wind, tide and wave.

The legacy of these erosive forces are wild beaches sculpted by the changing weather patterns of the seasons.

In certain places along the coast, the prevailing currents build up undulating hills of sand.
Down on the wetter sands, a tiny crab builds its shelter. As with most Australian habitats, the
coast is home to at least one member of the kangaroo family…

In the lee of offshore barriers, rich sediments form vast areas of mangrove forest and tidal flats. In these coastal zones, saltwater crocodiles are at the top of the food chain.

Mangroves survive in their salty environment by excreting salt through their leaves. Flooded mangrove forests provide an important nursery for many fish species. Birds such as pelicans are attracted to the richness of the mangrove systems.

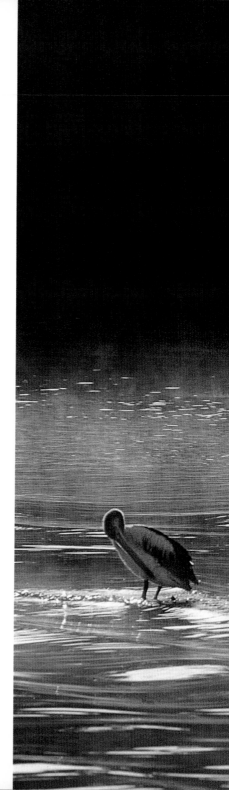

Creeks that snake their way through these intertidal zones provide perfect fishing grounds for birds of prey, such as the osprey. Least respected of coastal habitats, mangroves and tidal flats act as essential filters for runoff on its way to the sea…

Along parts of the tropical coast, the tangle of mangroves quickly gives way
to littoral rainforest, then to forested slopes and ranges. The giant tree frog is at home
in this transitional zone.

Winds laden with moisture from the sea dump their loads on the ranges, which are rich
in both plant and animal species. One inhabitant is the green python, which
starts its life in a bright yellow colour phase.

Streams flow from the mountains throughout the year. Pure, fresh water is the lifeblood of the rainforest.

Many of the mountains adjacent to the subtropical coast are also cloaked in rainforest.
The foliage of the canopy one day becomes the texture of the forest floor…

Boyd's forest dragon is an arboreal creature of the rainforest. Many rainforest trees have evolved buttressed roots to provide support and stability and to spread out across the soil in search of nutrients.

Strangler figs start their growth as tiny seedlings deposited high on a host tree. As the roots develop they descend around the host's trunk, encasing and eventually suffocating it. Fungi are one of the rainforests recyclers, helping to break down plant material into soil.

While epiphytes grow on other plants, they usually cause no harm to their hosts. Pied currawongs are known to raid the nests and feed on the young of other birds.

The dark igneous rock of this stream hints at the volcanic origins of many rainforest soils.
Penetrating rays reveal towering trees competing for light.

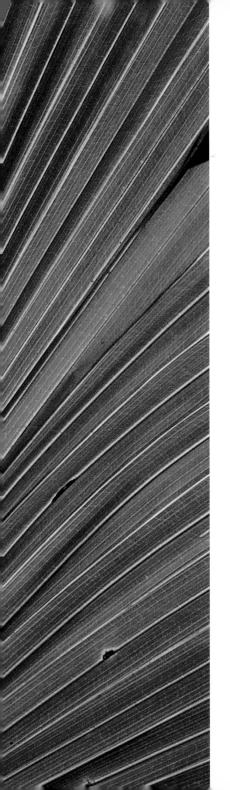

Palms are typical rainforest features. Cup moth larvae are brief but spectacular inhabitants of these forests.

Although tropical rainforest is often impenetrable from its margins, the large and flightless cassowary manages to make its home on the forest floor.

Brushtail possums are one of the many nocturnal creatures to inhabit these regions. Other special sights may lie concealed by mountainous terrain.

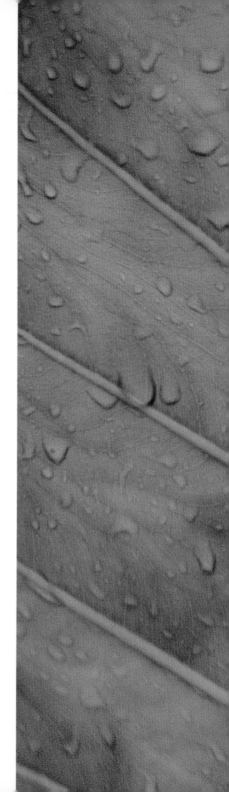

Loping flight takes the king parrot through the forest in search of young seed. Rainforest plants yield many natural remedies — the sap of the cunjevoi is thought to counteract the irritating effect of plants such as the giant stinging tree.

Rains come, once again bringing the sweet smell of renewal to the forest.
To the west of the coastal ranges, weather patterns are drier.

Pockets of lush vegetation remain in some sheltered areas, yet generally the habitats of the interior are drier, the forests more open.

Quiet pools have a life of their own. Platypus feed on bottom dwelling crustaceans and build their burrows into the bank.

Wood worms leave their distinctive trails under the bark of the scribbly gum.
Open forests and woodlands are home to a collection of Australia's plant icons, including
many of the 800 or more species of eucalyptus.

Largest of the kingfisher family, laughing kookaburras use their massive bill to subdue prey, including lizards and snakes. Koalas, on the other hand, enjoy a diet of gum leaves and daytime naps.

Evening light skims the underbelly of approaching weather. Such violent summer storms threaten to ignite the landscape.

Wildfires, fuelled by strong winds, race quickly through the dry forest. Some animals flee the flames, while others must shelter underground. In all but the most intense fires, established trees are only superficially affected...

Australia's unusual flora and fauna include grasstrees, which are fire tolerant and only flower after a burn, and marsupials, whose offspring do much of their development in their mother's pouch.

Grasslands, woodlands and forests are home to the dingo, Australia's only large, land-based predator.

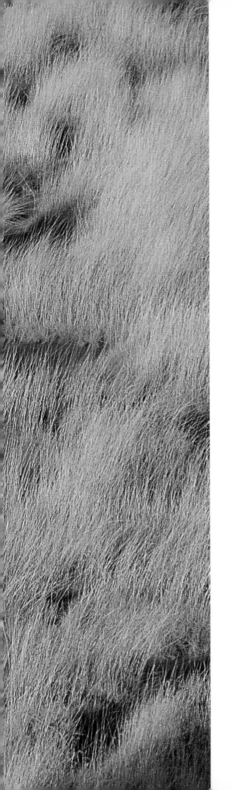

Spinifex grasslands cover more than one-fifth of the continent. The emu is a common sight on the vast plains of the interior.

Even in these drier regions, both land and sky are transformed into a sea of colour when birds such as this galah flock to waterholes or wildflowers spring up after quenching rains. Much of Australia's unique terrain is a product of the forces of nature and of time…

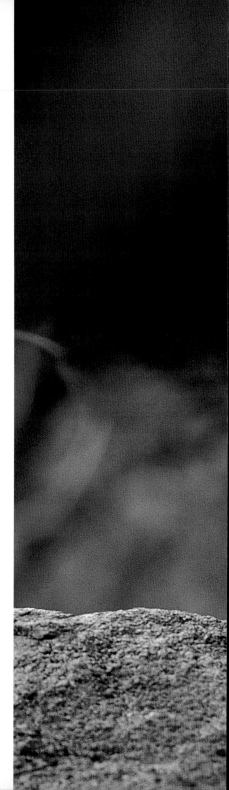

In central Australia huge mountain ranges have been weathered down into rock sculptures. The rocky slopes provide shelter for many species, such as the rock-wallaby which inhabits the caves and overhangs.

Millions of years of constant carving by the elements are responsible for the huge red rock islands of the centre. At home in this environment, male red kangaroos can weigh up to 85 kilograms.

Lizards have proven to be some of the most successful desert inhabitants. The central netted dragon finds a niche in these harsh surrounds.

Prevailing winds carry weathered debris across the interior, building vast sandy dunes.
The sand goanna is one of the desert's largest predators, growing
up to 1.6 metres in length.

Often dry for years at a time, some of the oldest riverbeds on earth meander through the desert. When food is hard to find, small carnivorous marsupials like the fat-tailed dunnart utilise stores of fat kept in their tails.

Ancient rivers have weathered gorges and canyons in the desert ranges. Trees cling to the canyon walls, their roots penetrating cracks in the rocky slopes.

Ant and termite mounds provide sustenance for the echidna. One of only two monotremes, or egg-laying mammals, the echidna uses its stout beak and strong front claws to probe deep into the mounds from which it extracts a meal with its sticky tongue.

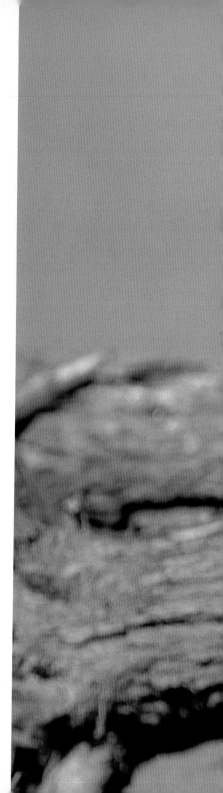

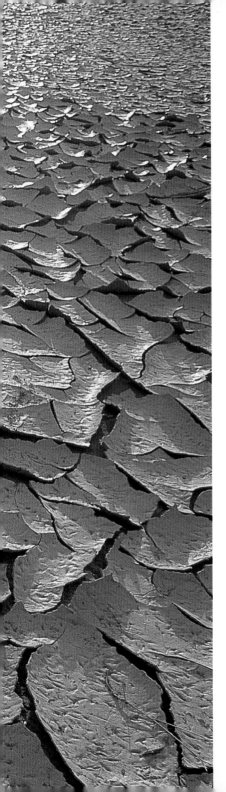

Claypans dry and crack as the last vestiges of moisture evaporate. Life-giving clouds pass overhead without yielding a drop.

At tropical latitudes, atmosphere and angled light have only a brief rendezvous
before darkness prevails…

PHOTOGRAPHER'S NOTES

To the many people who have provided me with assistance in the field, I am very grateful. I also wish to thank Paul Candlin, Jim McKitrick and John Hengelmolen for their encouragement, my wife Annette for her patience and my family for their support.

First published in Australia in 1998 by
New Holland Publishers (Australia) Pty Ltd
Sydney • London • Cape Town

14 Aquatic Drive Frenchs Forest NSW 2086 Australia

24 Nutford Place London W1H 6DQ United Kingdom

80 McKenzie Street Cape Town 8001 South Africa

National Library of Australia Cataloguing-in-Publication Data:

Jew, Darren.
Australia : reef, rainforest, red heart.

ISBN 1 86436 377 0.

1. Australia - Pictorial works. 2. Australia - Description and travel. I. Title.

919.400222

Publishing General Manager: Jane Hazell
Publisher: Averill Chase
Editor: Narelle Walford
Designer: Patricia McCallum
Reproduction and printing: Imago Productions, Singapore

Cover photographs: turtle hatchling; cunjevoi leaf; desert sands, Windorah, Queensland.